How to
Teach

How Students Learn
Fundamentals of Teaching
Preparation & Presentation
Evaluating Learning
Eliminating Gender Bias
Ethics

THE ART & SCIENCE
of Teaching

George P. Waldheim, Ed.D.

How to Teach

Disclaimer: This Handbook is a concise reference providing information essential to teaching both formal and informal groups including specialized schools, colleges, businesses, commercial, religious, public agencies, military, etc.—wherever the expectation is for a teacher to teach effectively so students learn. It is published under the expressed understanding that any decisions or actions taken as a result of reading this handbook must be based on your personal judgment and will be your sole responsibility. The author will not be held responsible for the consequences of any actions and/or decisions taken by others as a result of any information given or recommendations made.

Notes: The Examples described in this Handbook are all real as experienced by the author. The names, dates, and locations have been changed and/or omitted to protect privacy and identity. In addition, the terms "Teacher" and "Faculty" are used throughout this text to simplify the differing position titles of those teaching others.

DEDICATION

THIS IS A HANDBOOK DEDICATED to helping those who want to teach—teach. Many people are put in the position of having to teach without formal preparation—they search for help and this handbook is dedicated to them. It is also dedicated to those who are already teaching and want to improve their effectiveness.

The text in this Handbook is a concise reference providing information essential to teaching both formal and informal groups including specialized schools, colleges, businesses, commercial, religious, public agencies, military, etc.—wherever the expectation is for a teacher to teach effectively so students learn.

How to Teach promotes the Art and Science of teaching. The Art of developing effective teaching methods and the Science used to evaluate those methods and improve.

The fundamentals and methods presented in *How to Teach* are intended to prepare a teacher to ensure student learning and inspire the learning of those not learning.

It is a "primmer" on *How to Teach*.

TABLE OF CONTENTS

PREFACE

THE PURPOSE OF THIS HANDBOOK is to prepare a person to teach, and to teach effectively.

Teachers in elementary and high schools typically have a bachelor's degree (or higher) in their field of expertise and/or state approved credentials certifying them to teach. Teachers in Community Colleges, 4-year Colleges, and Universities have degree requirements in their individual areas of expertise but generally are not required to have education coursework or certification to teach. This handbook can prepare those who lack professional courses in teacher education, those who seek information in education as a career, and those who are already teaching and seek to improve their student's learning.

The goal of the information presented in this Handbook is to ensure student learning and inspire the learning of those less motivated to learning.

It is a "primmer" on *How to Teach.*

INTRODUCTION

"The mediocre teacher tells, the good teacher explains, the superior teacher demonstrates, the great teacher inspires" – William Ward

THE CONTENTS OF *HOW TO TEACH* include the following sequential Chapters:

- How Students Learn
- Fundamentals of Teaching
- Preparation & Presentation
- Evaluating Learning
- Eliminating Gender Bias
- Ethics

Knowing *How Students Learn* is essential to applying the *Fundamentals of Teaching*, used in the *Preparation & Presentation* of the subject being taught. The process of *Evaluating Learning* is used for improvement of instruction and grading. Additional Chapters, essential to teaching, are *Eliminating Gender Bias*, and *Ethics*.

The information presented in this Handbook

promotes the Art and Science of teaching. The Art of developing effective teaching methods and the Science used to evaluate those methods and improve.

It is a "primmer" on *How to Teach.*

Note: Because this is a working Handbook, blank pages are provided at the end of each Chapter for notes relative to the Chapter information and Chapter Tasks. The text presents information verbally thus completion of the Tasks are designed to involve the reader in the learning modes of Seeing and Feeling making the learning experience of the text multi-mode.

CHAPTER 1: HOW STUDENTS LEARN

It is logical that the responsibility of an effective teacher is to understand how students learn and then teach to the way the students learn. Effective teaching ensures student learning.

LEARNING

TO UNDERSTAND AND ENSURE LEARNING, teachers have to begin by asking and answering the age-old questions: How do we know something? How do we know we know something? How do we learn?

The following is a method, similar to that used in private business teaching programs, to describe how people receive and process information in their mind (beginning to learn). To start: Please think about the following statement you are about to read, then analyze the statement and put yourself mentally in the particular situation that the statement refers to. Here is the Statement:

"Remember the last time you were at the beach or the ocean."

Now examine the way you processed this thought. If you processed this information visually you probably saw a picture of the beach or ocean in your mind. If you did it through auditory you might have heard the waves etc. If you did it kinesthetically (feeling) you might have felt the hot sun. You may have also used a combination of these modes.

The following are typical conclusions: The strong majority of people received and processed the information visually because we have been receiving and processing information visually many more generations than we have been reading or concentrating on language interpretation. Biologically our physical system is more perfected towards Seeing (visual information reception and interpretation). As such, the Feeling (kinesthetic) mode would logically rank a biological second, and Hearing (auditory) third. In reality, what is the mode (learning method) most often used in teaching? Traditionally it is Hearing (auditory) which is comparatively less efficient in information receptivity. There are more effective ways to communicate information that just require planning to meet the receptive learning modes of *all* students.

LEARNING RECEPTION AND RETENTION

What process does a learner go through to not only put something into their mind, but then recall it from their mind, and then apply what is recalled? It would appear the whole notion of "learning" would have to include the aforementioned; putting something into one's mind, recalling it, and then applying it. One's varying ability to do that would then reflect a level of learning.

The most accepted research on learning says people put information into their minds by various combinations of Seeing, Feeling, and/or Hearing it. Although just Seeing, Feeling, and Hearing information does not in itself totally constitute learning. These are only the most common modes people use to communicate information into their, and/or others, minds. It is also accepted in teaching practice that if learners actually apply the information they Heard, Saw, and/or Felt, they tend to remember it better; meaning they could recall and apply it when needed, thus learned it. It is reasonable to expect that the more times learners applied the same information they heard, saw, and or felt, they would learn it to a greater level.

Modes of Learning in Schools

The Hearing mode of learning generally communicates information by verbal instruction (expounding, urging, telling) identified in this handbook as lecture-telling. This represents only one mode of learning.

The Seeing mode is typically promoted by using different media mechanisms such as a white board, computer screen, etc. These mechanisms really represent the Hearing mode; that is the learners are repeating to themselves what they are reading from the board or computer and thus Hear themselves.

The Feeling mode is left out of most teaching except for writing. Writing is ineffective as a representation of Feeling because as a person writes or presses keys they are concentrating on the spelling, the word, or groups of words written to complete the expression of their thought. Concentration is focused on the mechanics of the actual writing therefore "Feeling" relative to the topic is essentially non-existent and not remembered.

Teaching-learning will be significantly improved by applying more effective modes of Seeing and Feeling. In addition, it is well documented that people naturally receive and process information at different levels of reception via the three modes. Some do well with Seeing, versus others who do better with Feeling, versus others with Hearing, even though individuals tend to use one to all three abilities combined. *Overall people tend to use all three modes to receive and process information although individually have differing, and in many cases significant, personal biases utilizing those modes.* This has a remarkable effect on learning and reinforces the logic of teaching to the way students learn.

The Learning Dilemma

A learning dilemma is created in the classroom when mainly using the lecture-telling (Hearing) teaching method.

A learner who is more biased in the Seeing or Feeling modes of information reception naturally creates mental pictures or feelings of the verbal statements made by the teacher. As the telling continues the biased learner is concentrating on the mental pictures or feelings and is attentively missing (not absorbing) the remaining telling, creating a dilemma. The dilemma is between the mental pictures and/or the verbal information—not retaining both at the same time. Explanation: "Neurological science has demonstrated that the human brain is incapable of focusing on two things at once." Naturally creating mental pictures or feelings in one's mind from lecture-telling sentences diverts from retaining subsequent verbiage thus the biased learner is prone to missing information. It is apparent that those biased learners suffer the consequence of receiving and concentrating on information differently when only sent verbally thus creating a receptive distraction and uncertain learning (information retention).

This situation means that a large number of students will not escape their biological tendency towards receiving and retaining information through Seeing and Feeling and are subject to the dilemma created by lecture-telling. *Their learning will tend to be inversely proportional (opposite) to the strength of their bias.* This receptive diversion affects so many learners/students and could be drastically resolved by teaching to the way students learn—making learning easier rather than more difficult.

Classroom experience verifies that the number of *significantly* verbally biased learners tends to be small which indicates that the larger number of remaining learners will be variably affected by the Learning Dilemma. Knowing this reality should motivate a conscientious teacher to improve their teaching methods to include all the modes of learning.

> It is only logical that learners would receive and retain information more effectively if all three modes were used to send it. That is an important basis for effective instruction. In other words, teachers can reach more students, more effectively, utilizing all three modes

The learning dilemma is intensified when only using the lecture-telling (Hearing) teaching method. This generally produces a wide range of test grades described as the learning variance within the class *(conventional spread of grades A to F).*

Contrary to this is that those learners with the stronger receptive learning modes of Seeing and Feeling are in learning difficulty right from the start. They tend to include the learners who return to school after being in the world of work, proving they can learn by using the other modes of Seeing and Feeling; and because they were successful, why can't they go back to school and do well, in spite of their prior experience? Many do, and tend to do it very well.

In explanation: It is apparent that the Seeing and Feeling biased learners have significantly experienced converting on-the-job Hearing information into Seeing and Feeling (Doing) applications at work and thus were more successful learning (putting information into their mind, recalling, and applying it) than they ever were at school. *They learned to learn from how they learn.*

LEARNING WITH THE LEARNING DILEMMA

Those learners who have learning mode biases more related to Seeing and Doing versus Hearing have to reinforce their learning by recalling the missed information through notes, reading, discussion, and then study the missed information in order to gain a better understanding (learning). The learners separate the information and review it in their minds by reading or listening—trying to visualize it (Seeing) and/or visualizing the application of it (Doing) for memory retention. Thus, conversional learning takes additional time and makes learning more difficult. In addition, conversional learning is very contingent on one's interest in the subject. The more interested the more motivated to learning—and the converse. With little interest the learners tend not to focus on conversional learning but instead they tend to memorize it just for the test. Thus, the learner "only knows" the information for the immediate test, forgoing long term retention.

By teaching to the way all students learn, utilizing all the modes of learning, learning is made easier and the grading reflects higher information retention.

In review: Utilizing the lecture-telling (Hearing) teaching method alone forces the strong majority of students in the class to mentally convert the lecture material to their individual biases in order to understand or learn what is being taught. The students have to adjust their learning from the way the teacher teaches. It behooves the teacher to teach to the particular way the students learn, thereby avoiding the additional time and mental conversions the students have to make in order to convert the material to their receptive wavelengths. They would learn the information easier.

The learning adjustments students have to make are also determined by their motivation—fueled by their interest. Without interest, the biased learning mode students will forgo their effort in the conversion process and tend to test poorly.

Today's learners appear to respond significantly different from learners just a few years ago. The technology ease and speed of making large amounts of information available has drastically changed the attention span of most people. If it interests them, they continue to read and or see on. If not, they hit mental delete and move on to the next item of initial interest. This conditioning directly relates to the learning behavior of the student in the classroom. If they are interested in the topic presented, and they are biased in the mode of presentation, they will definitely do better than those disinterested will and/or biased otherwise. The real key here is if they are interested. If not interested, regardless of their learning mode bias, they will probably tend to tune out the presentation and focus some of their thoughts elsewhere, not able to receive and retain enough information to start the recall and application process of learning. Since the attention span of the learner today is so much shorter than that of previous years, it is necessary for the effective teacher to develop interest in the topic right from the start relative to any concepts and/or topics they are presenting.

Teaching, according to various dictionary definitions, is "to impart knowledge" and/or "to cause to learn." This has initiated learning problems by only imparting knowledge through verbal lecture-telling. If students remember it okay, and if not? In today's current world that does not work well. Attitude, time available, family structure, interest, environment, etc. are all affecting factors.

To be an effective teacher one has the responsibility

to impart knowledge in the most effective way. The improvements in teaching methods that effective teachers have to make to ensure student learning is an essential part of this handbook.

> Effective teaching ensures learning.

HOW TO ENSURE LEARNING

First: Develop an interest in the required topic. Find a way to show the learner how it will affect them in an important way.

One sentence as to the relevance of the topic doesn't work. Most people's attention is gained when the nature of the topic affects something important to them. Incidentally, threatening to give students an "F" grade does not promote interest and may actually promote the reverse. Topics necessary to be presented in classrooms or elsewhere generally have a beginning point. Someone discovered that knowledge somewhere and for some purpose of interest. Example: Where and/or Why did the subject of Algebra develop? Where and/or Why the Pythagorean Theorem? Where and/or Why does a minus times a minus equal a plus, etc.? These beginning points, Where and/or Why, can be of interest to learners;

especially when related to how they seriously affect those learners today. People, even students, have to have a reason to want to do something. Learning something one sees no purpose in is a lost endeavor, defeated before starting, and verbal lecture-telling without convincing purpose, is very successful at that.

Second: Teach all topics utilizing all three receptive modes of learning: Seeing, Feeling, and Hearing. A lot of forethought, known as pre-preparation, will have to go into the ethical design and implementation of this. The importance of this cannot be over stressed. Even if interested, if learners do not receive information on their wavelength many will be lost and/or experience greater difficulty in learning.

Example: The person who said their elementary grade teacher was having trouble with the students understanding the process of averaging numbers gave an example of the power of all three modes. In desperation, the teacher marched the whole class to the school gym where they had the final scores of all their school's basketball games posted on the wall. The subsequent teaching and learning is obvious—"Seeing" the actual scores posted, "Feeling" what it is like to be on the court where the scores actually occurred, and gaining a real life experience by actually manipulating (averaging) the score numbers viewed, where they occurred, in order to envision the future scores of their team. The important point here was twofold. The teacher engaged the students in all three modes of learning (teacher said he could see the light bulbs light up in the student's eyes) and the result was an adult who never forgot the experience, and the learning that took place because of it.

The variances in individual student's modes of learning, as well as the changing interest of individual students at the time of learning, is unpredictable. Therefore, the most effective way to teach is to prepare and present the reference material multi-mode.

> Presenting information not utilizing the three receptive modes is less effective because it restricts the natural learning abilities of students.

Third: Evaluate (test) for recall and application of the topic, then analyze the scores. The test should indicate students have learned the topic when:

- They remember it.
- They remember how to do it.
- They do it.
- They repeat it.

The level at which they accomplish these steps will identify their level of learning (poor to excellent)—the goal being higher grades and less dispersion of grades A to F for all students in the class (More A to C grades with less or no D to F's).

The purpose of evaluation is improvement of instruction. Analyzing learning, after testing, will show the teacher what teaching deficiencies may or may not exist (variance of test scores) determined by the modes of learning. This gives the teacher the opportunity to improve the modes of learning—if necessary and serves as the teacher's self-check. It is a necessary part of the teacher's instructional improvement.

Fourth: Decide to not record the grades (not needed as the evaluation was a sub-topic etc.), record the grades as documentation of the level of learning of the topic objective, or improve the teaching methods, utilizing all three learning modes, and re-teach—re-evaluating again for grading.

The overall class results of the grading, personal names withheld, should be readily available information to be used for comparative improvement purposes.

Recall all the great teachers in history. They all seem to follow the pattern of effective teaching previously outlined. They always developed interest in their various teachings which set the stage for learning.

Their teachings were filled with Seeing and Feeling experiences, so much so that books thousands of years later still describe them. They even evaluated and repeated the application of their recipient's learning in numerous ways.

In Schools and Colleges, almost all effective teachers have similar things in common. Their first concern is always student learning. Even the students know it; they feel it. They are hands-on, they most often develop instruction using the three modes, and their student evaluations reflect their efforts. Few failures, if any, and always the highest perceived student evaluations. Their subjects even include Math and Chemistry, traditionally known for high levels of difficulty. In order to improve learning teachers must teach to ensure learning. Anything less is diminishing the students' opportunity to learn.

> The only failure in the classroom is the teacher.

LEARNING BY PERCEPTION

Students are much more, or significantly more, perceptive than most educators give them credit for. They know and respond to the attitude, personality, and persona the teacher displays, consciously and/or unconsciously. Why is it that a seemingly small frail mature teacher can hold a class of 35 plus energetic combined gender students spellbound and attentive versus the opposite person's physical stature, with opposite results? The students' perception of the teacher and their resultant behavior must be in reaction to whatever the teacher displays, does, or has done. A student's perception of non-verbal teacher characteristics is much more related to their classroom behavior than one can imagine. If students perceive and believe teachers are concerned about their individual learning, then their attitude towards accepting or learning what is being taught appears to be more instinctively motivated, or more positively influenced. This leads one to believe their level of learning will be greater. On the other hand, if a teacher is extremely effective in delivering the information being taught, but the students' perception of the teacher is threatening or impersonal, then the level of learning might be decreased from what it could and/or should be.

The influence of the teacher's personal commitment to their individual learning, as perceived and believed by students, is one of the most learning related motivational factors in the classroom. It is something very difficult to be taught for a teacher to do. It appears almost intrinsic to the character, personality, persona, and commitment of the person teaching. Excellent teachers have it. That is why many excellent teachers often appear to do their job in spite of financial issues—they love their job responsibility (student learning) and the students know, believe, and are motivated to learn because of it. This characteristic of excellent teachers is so common and would be difficult to be taught by any teacher education programs. Excellent teachers have it; others have to work harder to try to display/achieve it. Students, as well as others, react to what they See, Feel, and Hear—in that order. *Sound familiar?*

CHAPTER REVIEW

How Students Learn: The most accepted research on learning indicates that people put information into their minds by various combinations of Seeing, Feeling, and/or Hearing. It is also accepted in teaching practice that if learners actually apply the information they Saw, Felt, and/or Heard they would tend to remember it better; meaning they could recall and apply it when needed, thus learned it. It is reasonable to expect that the more times learners applied the same information they Saw, Felt, and/or Heard they would learn it to a greater level.

Ensure student learning by First developing an interest

in the topic. Second: teach all topics by utilizing all three receptive learning modes. Third: Analyze learning by testing for recall and application of the topic. Review the variance of the test scores for improvements if necessary. Fourth: improve teaching methods if necessary (possibly re-teach) and re-evaluate again for grading.

Students also learn by perception: responding to the attitude, personality, and persona the teacher displays.

CHAPTER 1 TASKS

Create:

▶ genuine student interest in all course topics and abolish threats of any kind.

▶ all three effective learning modes for teaching each course topic.

▶ evaluations (tests) to measure and analyze student learning of course topics.

▶ improvement in teaching methods.

▶ a classroom perception that the teacher's primary priority is student learning.

Tasks Note: By completing the chapter Tasks, utilizing all three modes of learning, the reader will improve their ability to ensure student learning.

Chapter 1 Reference: "The Impossibility of Focusing on Two Things at Once" MIT Sloan Management Review. Morela Hernandez.

Notes:

Notes:

CHAPTER 2: FUNDAMENTALS OF TEACHING

It has been said that if you want to change the world, then teach. Teachers teach, students learn, then students go out in the world and apply what they have learned. The more effective the teaching, the more effective the student, the more change that takes place.

RESPONSIBILITY

IT IS LOGICAL TO JUDGE teaching, and the effectiveness of teaching, on the extent of student learning. It would be vague and misleading to conclude that the foremost responsibility of a teacher is just to "teach." In daily usage the term "teach" has become more a figure of speech used to represent many differing perceptions, deflecting from its primary purpose: student learning.

How is the verb "teach" defined? Dictionary examples include "to impart knowledge," "to bestow," "to give instruction," or more specifically, "to cause to learn." The real message in the definition of the verb "teach," is that something happens because of it; teachers are imparting, bestowing, giving, etc. *How are teachers imparting, bestowing, giving, etc., or—how well are students learning?* What is the ultimate outcome of the process of teaching? It logically must be student learning. That is the very reason teachers are teaching—so students learn.

It is a reality that teaching causes student learning to take place therefore teachers are fundamentally responsible for student learning.

In many instances one can teach and give instruction but that does not ensure student learning. This is the dilemma and challenge in teaching. This Handbook is written to remedy that challenge.

> The teacher's fundamental responsibility is student learning.

Improving Learning

Learning happens in an environment of varying student abilities, interests, dispositions, feelings, etc., much of which is in reaction to teaching. If teaching is improved then learning will improve, as well as the student perception and value of learning.

To improve the level of student learning means improving the way students are able to learn. The single learning mode of Hearing is most effective with those learners who more naturally absorb enough information heard and remembered from the lecturer to pass informational tests on the lecture and move on easier in the system. This selective teaching practice (lecture-telling) is maintained by the inferences drawn from the test scores; high scores are inferred to represent high student effort/learning and the low scores just the opposite. **In reality, the grades more logically represent the varying strengths of individual students' modes of learning: Hearing, Seeing, and Doing.**

Effective teachers improve learning by teaching to the learning modes of the whole class—Seeing, Doing, and Hearing. They then evaluate at what level the students have learned the class material and make changes, if necessary, to the teaching methods (modes of learning) in order to improve learning the next time the topic is taught. The important point will be the level of student learning considered acceptable by analyzing what the students have learned in the class versus what the students were supposed to have learned in that class. The goal being higher grades and less dispersion of the grades (A to F) for all the students in the class.

Teaching, using all the student's learning modes (Seeing, Doing, Feeling), tends to improve the learning of those not learning. This is the responsibility of an effective teacher—teaching to the way students learn. It is well accepted that students have learned when:

- They remember it.
- They remember how to do it.
- They do it.
- They repeat it.

COMBINING TEACHING
AND TRAINING

The single mode of teaching (Hearing and Reading) has historically been applied in more academic and knowledge based courses (theoretical and abstract); versus training (Seeing and Doing) which is hands on practical and is perceived as adding skills onto existing knowledge. This traditionally accepted view of these two distinct types of education is now effectively altered by the digital information age. Today academic subjects, out of necessity, have to be taught with both theoretical knowledge and application skills together. For liberal arts, professional, and technical education, the subjects include varying levels of abstract mathematics, science, language, etc. and the necessary application of those abstract concepts. The distinction between Teaching and Training is now blended because of the necessity to understand the theoretical concepts as well as perform their use. Students, instead of just memorizing for the test, now ask Why? and How? and expect to see some relevance to what they learn. Teachers have to develop the skills for the applications of the knowledge they are teaching. Without teaching the application skills, that promotes self-interest, the student attention span is reduced and so is learning.

Teaching must include the learning methods of Seeing and Doing. Knowledge is perceived by the educational consumer to be dead-end without the ability to apply it. Successful learning requires knowing that you know something by being able to use it. This reality, the general educational consumer needing the application skills, is promoting a fundamental evolution in traditional Teaching versus Training by combining the learning modes of Seeing, Feeling, and Hearing.

IMPROVING STUDENT RETENTION

When a teacher plans and teaches using all the learning receptivity modes including Seeing (observing reality), Feeling (applying by doing), and Hearing (listening and reading) with the intent that all students must learn; the results tend to modify the typical grading inferences (large A to F dispersion), and thus the justification for selective teaching by verbal lecture and descriptive reading. It is teaching directed to all students by utilizing all of the most common learning receptivity modes to acquire knowledge. The only variables remaining are the differences in the individual student's level of information retention; they all are able to receive and process information, but retain it at different levels. Logically the graded scores would be higher because more students receive/process the information; **thus, more learn easier.**

Single mode teaching, verbal lecture including reading, unwittingly results in the students being graded on how well they adapt to the verbal lecturing and those that do not adapt are eliminated from the system by low grades, and/or dropping out. The results of this do not disappear because years later those Seeing and Doing biased students eliminated from the system tend to come back and do very well, many in similar classrooms, and the rhetoric/justification is they are "more mature now." More accurately they were disinterested because of ineffective learning (learning dilemma); resultantly the information was incomplete so they didn't understand/retain it, and because of that they lost interest and were perceived as poor students. The reality is that those students are usually the students who return to school after being in the world of work, finding they can learn by converting on-the-job "Hearing" information into

Seeing and Doing applications at work and because they were successful, they go back to school and do well in spite of their prior academic experiences.

Greater application of fundamental teaching methods will have a positive effect on retaining students in school rather than unwittingly causing students to do poorly or drop out—only to have them *learn how to learn,* and then return.

IMPROVING LEARNING REINFORCEMENT

To teach more effectively to all students, utilizing all three modes of learning receptivity, requires analysis and improvement in teaching methods. Conventional practice is to assign student homework as learning re-inforcement. In reality, the homework is generally the same verbal learning mode of teaching (students hearing themselves read) emphasizing an unwitting practice that more verbal learning is better for *all.* This is positive reinforcement to those biased towards the Hearing mode of learning but actually promotes negative learning re-inforcement to those more receptive to the Seeing and Feeling modes. Because the homework is not on their "wavelength" (even more difficult to learn at home than in class) those not as receptive to the Hearing mode struggle and become much more perceptively discouraged and disinterested, thus they drop-out or survive with low grades.

> Incorporating all three modes of learning for all course objectives should be a fundamental part of teaching in class, as well as assigned instruction.

The reality is that the Seeing and Feeling biased students have had to learn to adapt to the single learning mode of Hearing. They have displayed and proven an exceptionally strong commitment in spite of their learning dilemma. Given the fundamental responsibility of the teacher being "student learning" it is logical to teach to the way students learn thus improving the learning of those not learning.

CHAPTER REVIEW

Fundamentals of Teaching: Teaching, using all the student's learning modes (Seeing, Doing, Feeling), reaches all the students and improves the learning of those not learning. This is fundamental to effective teaching—teaching to the way students learn.

Effective teachers evaluate at what level the students have learned the class material and make changes, if necessary, to the teaching methods (modes of learning) in order to improve learning the next time the topic is taught. The important point will be the level of student learning considered acceptable by analyzing what the students have learned in the class versus what the students were supposed to have learned in that class. The goal being higher grades and less dispersion of the grades (A to F); for all the students in the class.

Improve teaching and training, student retention, and learning reinforcement by applying all the learning receptivity modes of Seeing (observing reality), Feeling (applying by doing), and Hearing (listening and reading) with the intent that all students learn. ***The fundamental responsibility of the teacher is student learning.***

Chapter 2 Tasks

Plan how to:

▶ accept the fundamental teaching responsibility of student learning.

▶ combine abstract learning and training of course topics.

▶ improve student retention.

▶ improve learning reinforcement.

Tasks Note: By completing the chapter Tasks, utilizing all three modes of learning, the reader will improve their ability to ensure student learning.

Notes:

Notes:

Chapter 3: Preparation & Presentation

Experience of effective teachers has proven that preparation is the most important step in teaching. "If preparation is inadequate the results will be poor levels of learning characterized by a number of disruptive student situations."

Preparation for Presentation is a habit of successful people who plan their work; then work their plan.

Preparation

The Lesson Plan

By definition "teaching imparts knowledge; learning acquires knowledge." **How to Teach** successfully, to the way students acquire knowledge (student's modes of learning), necessitates pre-planning individual lessons—thus the Lesson Plan. This Plan (limited to one page) is a concise record of the reference material to teach, the topic objective, teaching methods (modes of learning), an analysis of learning, and improvement (if necessary). The five parts of the Lesson Plan are described as follows:

- Reference Material
- Topic Objective
- Teaching Methods
- Analysis of Learning
- Improvement

Reference Material

It is necessary to identify (on the Lesson Plan) the reference material being used by the teacher to form the contents of the lesson. If a book or written material, indicate the name, location (pages), etc. so that it can be found for any subsequent change, review, improvement, etc. The reference material contains the knowledge the students are expected to learn. It is the content of the course.

Topic Objective

The next step in preparation is to divide the reference material or lesson information into Topic Objectives. The most important information to be learned should be represented by stated/written objectives; the reason for teaching the topic. Call it what whatever: objectives, results, aims, purposes, reasons, etc. The knowledge to be learned should be represented by a statement describing the resulting expectations of what is being taught—what the learner should be able to do as a result of the teaching methods used.

The course or body of knowledge that the teacher is responsible for should be represented by these topic objectives. This means reviewing the course textbook or written content and writing the objectives. When written, the Topic Objectives represent the initial pre-planned stepped outcomes of the course and should be measurable to determine the student's level of learning.

In many instances the teacher will receive a new textbook or course material too late to preview and write the objectives. At that point the only alternative is to proceed writing the objectives and the Lesson Plan as the class schedule continues—prior to each class meeting. Sometimes textbooks have objectives clearly stated so a review could utilize those objectives ensuring that the learner's performance of those objectives can be measured or revised to be measured.

Example: At the end of this (lesson, session, topic, etc.) the learner should be able to correctly (perform, complete, compute, solve, etc.)…the actual purchase price of a discounted item given the various methods of store discounting without the use of a calculator.

Example: As a result of this… the learner should be able to accurately interpret the author's meanings…

Example: At the end of this… the learner should be able to correctly solve a problem containing …

Example: As a result of this… the learner should be able to both accurately investigate and verbally communicate the…

These examples state the objective of the teaching; what the learner should be able to know and perform as a result of the teaching effort. It is the most important step in preparation of teaching and is the necessary starting point; describing what the learner should be able to do—the expected result.

Without Topic Objectives, teaching to ensure learning and subsequent improvement will be next to impossible to document and achieve. Therefore, each Topic Objective should be recorded as the 2nd major item in the teacher's one page Lesson Plan. This is the written outline for that particular lesson session, thus the course will be made up of cumulative one page Lesson Plans.

Important Note: Do not overload your course or lesson sessions with Topic Objectives. Objectives should only represent major topics in the course and should be made up of lesser steps. Keep the Objectives general enough that its parts are measurable by testing. It is not uncommon to only have a very small number of Objectives per chapter of a course text. Limit could be no more than one Objective per class session or one per a number of class sessions.

Teaching Methods

It is the preparation of the Teaching Methods (modes of learning) that will determine how well the learners receive the information presented. Remember that individuals receive and process information via the three most common modes: Seeing, Feeling, and Hearing. If a teacher decides to only verbally teach then they are reaching those biased to Hearing and creating a learning dilemma for those receptive otherwise. To be on the receptive wavelength of all students the teachers must present the information utilizing all three modes. To do this requires that the one most familiar with the subject matter, the teacher, develop strategies to accomplish this. What is it that the teacher can ethically invent, develop, present, involve students in, etc. that compels the learner to not only hear, but to see and feel the subject matter effects of the topic being taught? Seeing would involve utilizing experiences from various traditional media methods to real life visual applications. Receiving information through feeling involves experiencing physical involvement, reactions, applications, movement, doing, etc. Examples of teaching methods involving all the modes of learning are around us in everyday life. One only has to ethically relate similar processes to the classroom. Whether a student is to learn a mathematical formula, chemical procedure, geographical term, language grammar, philosophical concept, poetry, etc., it is more effective to see the topic objective applied, in addition to actually applying it. This is essential to ensure learning.

Example: Students to bring to class (examples only) of items advertised to be purchased by a consumer at whatever discount offered and use each item as examples to learn how to determine the actual purchase price (topic objective) etc. The students are involved in Seeing and Doing with example items as they learn solutions for: percentage discounts, two for one, buy one half off the other, etc.

Another mode of learning improvement was in teaching the non-visual internal structure of a metallic material; an abstract/theoretical subject. The lecture-telling scenario was to draw the internal molecular structure on the white board and verbally describe the physical changes (dimensions and hardness) of the structure versus temperature changes. Student testing always produced mixed levels of results. As part of analyzing the test grades, versus the topic objective, improvement in the teaching method was obvious and necessary in order to improve student learning. Thus, a real-life demonstration of the actual effects of the molecular change in the material was developed.

Improvement: Actual   metallic   material   was

heated (safety precautions taken) to documented temperature levels and cooled both rapidly and/or slowly so the students could visually see and test the different physical changes (dimensions and hardness) in the material versus the different rates of cooling.

Almost every time that real-life demonstration was performed (to a class of 35 to 45 students) some student always yelled out appreciatively: "that's what my chemistry teacher meant." Ironically, many teachers were taught the same concept verbally and never really understood the concept until they experienced it, by seeing it, in real life applications. Seeing the application of a concept is believing. The methodology was also extended by having students investigate examples of the concept application outside of the classroom and report back their findings. This represented the feeling mode of learning and was verified by almost always 100 percent level of learning response to the testing of that topic objective; a significant improvement from prior learning of that objective.

The Teaching Methods (modes of learning) developed by a teacher will be unique to each person teaching the topic assigned. A teacher's experience, knowledge, demeanor, etc. may dictate the way this is done. It should be developed for each objective, recorded as part of the learning plan, and continuously improved through analysis of the student's level of learning versus the modes of learning. Again, this is a necessary part of the Teaching Plan and is the part most essential to improvement.

Analysis of Learning

Evaluate (test) for recall and application of the topic, then analyze the scores. The test should indicate students have learned the topic when:

- They remember it.
- They repeat it.
- They remember how to do it.
- They do it.

The level at which students accomplish these steps will identify their level of learning (poor to excellent). The goal is higher grades and less dispersion of grades A to F for all students in the class. More A to C grades with less or no D to F grades.

The purpose of evaluation (testing) is improvement of instruction. The evaluation after the teaching process is to show the teacher what deficiencies may or may not exist (variance of test scores) in the pre-planned modes of learning. This gives the teacher the opportunity to analyze the scores and serves as a teacher self-check. It is a necessary part of the teacher's instructional improvement.

Record the type of test or tests that are used to determine the level of learning of the Topic Objective being tested. Include the numerical method of the scoring range; A to F percentages. This information is necessary for review and analysis when improving the Teaching Methods. Testing is necessary to evaluate the student's level of learning of each topic objective and serves as the basis for improvement, if necessary, for the next time the objective is taught.

To get to the point where you are reading this text it is realized that you have had experience in testing; if not as a teacher, certainly as a student. Therefore, most readers are familiar with written essay, computer formats, multiple choice, and practical applications as they are the most common test experiences in the education system.

Example: Students responding by computer to multiple questions of lecture-telling is the very nature of testing verbal learning. Good for verbal learners; others not so good. Effective teachers have found that there are many other methods of evaluating the levels of learning and some actually involve learning while evaluating.

Example: Giving portions of questions to small groups of students, made up from a large class, with the goal of having each small group work to verbally agree on answers to their assigned questions. Then, have each group present their answers verbally in the large class meeting until all groups were heard and involved in the derivation of those answers. After that learning experience evaluate (test) for the level of learning of the topic objective.

The important point in testing is to determine how well (at what level) *all* the students learned the material and then use that data to improve, if necessary, the modes of learning for the next time the topic is taught.

Improvement

The teacher has multiple options regarding Grading: Either decide not to record the grades (not needed as the evaluation was a sub-topic etc.), record the grades as documentation of the level of learning of the topic objective, or improve the teaching methods, utilizing all three learning modes, and re-teach—re-evaluating again for grading. The overall class results of the grading, personal names withheld, should be readily available information to be used for comparative improvement purposes.

The analysis of class grades resulting from the lecture (Hearing) mode of learning typically ranges from effective learning high scores to non-effective learning low scores. It is obvious to ensure learning of all students in the class that low scores indicate an immediate and necessary improvement in the methods of instruction—even to the point of re-teaching the topic objective.

Even with the variance in student groups it seems reasonable to accept the concept that learning will improve with most teaching method improvements. This is readily apparent from analyzing grades, resulting from improvements in the modes of learning evolved over many classes.

The foremost challenge of the teacher is not to try to change the students, but to improve the teaching methods which in turn will improve the level of learning of the students.

This is the real-world proven concept of analysis and improvement and appears to be standard practice for those perceived as excellent teachers.

Realistic examples of needed improvement are apparent when a topic objective is taught utilizing the verbal methodology only. Testing usually reveals who the better verbal learners are and those who are not. The grades achieved will make these distinctions readily apparent. Improving the teaching methods, utilizing all the learning modes of Seeing, Feeling, and Hearing, should result in quite different learning and grading results. Instead of the grades being skewed in favor of the more natural verbal learners, the grades tend to portray a more uniform and higher level of Learning for all—more students learn easier and thus better.

In reality, the Analysis of Learning shows the teacher how effective the teaching methods were and thus is documented justification for planning improved methods if needed. The improved methods become the modes of learning the next time the topic objective is taught, and so on, thus continuing improvement in learning.

Another reason to document improved teaching methods is related to one's teaching performance evaluation. Teaching plans are documented examples of improvement and can serve to positively justify re-appointment and/or continued employment. It not only says that "I am doing my job," but documents credible effort to continuously improve student learning—the most important responsibility of the teacher. One often hears the statement that "the best job insurance is to make yourself so valuable to your employer that they cannot afford to be without you." Under normal circumstances it is difficult to imagine an educational organization divesting itself of well documented effective teachers. Lesson Plans are an excellent investment in improving student learning as well as documenting professional performance. The very nature of successful improvement is derived from the well proven axiom: "Plan your work first, then work your plan."

In Review: The complete Lesson Plan has five essentials: the Course Reference Material, Topic Objective, Teaching Methods, Analysis of Learning, and Improvement. The Lesson Plan should be taken to each class session as a guide, record, and self-check on the application of the Topic Objective and modes of learning.

The lesson reference material itself (information to be taught relative to each topic objective) is separate from the Lesson Plan and can take traditional forms such as textbooks, notes, documents, etc., from which the objectives are derived. The way the reference material topics are presented in class is determined by the pre-planned modes of learning. The teacher will naturally refer to the Lesson Plan and the reference material as the class session progresses.

An example format for a Lesson Plan is provided on the next page. This can be used for each topic objective of the course. It is the teacher's plan to ensure student learning and promote improvement.

Example: **Lesson Plan   No.____**

Course: **Teacher:**   **Date:**

Reference Material: *text name or reference, page numbers, special items, course information sheets, etc.*

Topic Objective: *what the learner should be able to do*

Teaching Methods: *modes of learning*
  Seeing   *visual*

  Doing   *applying*

  Hearing *listening/reading*

Analysis of Learning: *tests, dispersion of grades, analysis*

Improvement: *modes of learning for next time*

PRESENTATION

1st Meeting

When first meeting the group of new learners an instructional process to follow should include the following: Who, What, Where, When, and Why. The completed first Lesson Plan can be used as a guide for much of the information needed. In some organizations (schools etc.) multiple course related information is pre prepared on a single or multiple page handout.

The following are items related to the course that are typically covered in the initial meeting.

Who: It is Important for the teacher to first introduce themself and indicate how they want to be addressed; Mr., Mrs., Ms., Dr., etc. By doing this the students will have the correct pronunciation of the teacher's name and will feel easier about referring to the teacher for questions and future communication. Additionally, the teacher may ask the individuals in the group to introduce themselves—if the group size is small enough (up to 23 or 30), otherwise any larger group would tend to be too time consuming, repetitive, might become a little disruptive, and thus counterproductive.

What: Use the Lesson Plan to clarify the reference information the group will be learning. If a text—the information about the text. If other—the information of the material and its origin. Also, what specialized equipment might be needed, supplies, etc. More information about the course might include grading, homework, group work, special assignments, due dates, etc.

Where: The meeting locations should be clarified as to where the class will meet. This is important as many students have differing travel methods/obligations and students coming and going will need to make their travel arrangements.

When: The times of the class start and stop are very important because students coming and going at differing times throughout the class session is disruptive and must be avoided.

It is best to clarify attendance obligations at the initial meeting.

Why: This is the point in the class session where the teacher can use the visual (Seeing) mode of learning to convince the Learners how the course goal or first topic objective relates and affects them individually. When something directly affects a person individually; that promotes attention relative to its level of importance. The more important the effect of the topic to the learner the more attention it will receive.

Subsequent Class Meetings

The Lesson Plan for each session should be the guide as to that session's Topic Objective, the Reference

Material to be covered as well as the Teaching Methods. Initially the class should begin with the visual mode of learning, convincing as to why the topic relates and affects the learner individually, creating a stronger interest in the need for the information. After that, presenting the reference material (text) information utilizing the three modes of learning—Seeing, Doing, and Hearing. Prior to the end of each session a review of the information covered should be accomplished possibly through question and answer or other techniques that the teacher can guide.

Complimenting the Use of Textbooks

Traditionally textbooks are the accepted source of "how to," and are used by the teacher as the informational guide for the subject being taught. Authors have extensive knowledge of the material they are presenting in the text although sometimes this can limit learning. For instance, an author who too briefly emphasizes the importance or application and focuses on the mechanics of the concept itself. The experts in their field write the texts used in courses and spend most of the text on the mechanics of whatever they are presenting. Introductory paragraphs or explanations rarely explain convincingly why and how this affects and interests the reader. The experts are focused on the mechanics of the presentation, which rightfully is of great interest to them, whereby the basic motivation is generally thought to be expected rather than needed to be generated. This is where the teacher must compliment and expand interest in the topics of the text and not ignore what seems academic to them.

Textbook learning should be reinforced by the teacher's ingenuity to create multi-mode learning experiences of the author's intentions. Textbooks are an excellent guide, but the real responsibility for student learning lies with the teacher's interpretation and created learning experiences to accomplish the textbook intentions. The real challenge of the teacher is not to change the students but to improve the teaching methods which in turn will improve the student's level of learning.

Developing the Interest to Learn

What does the teacher have to do to promote student learning? In addition to creating the learning objectives for individual topics, the methods of teaching, documenting and evaluating the student learning of those objectives, it is a fundamental responsibility of the teacher to generate "the cause to learn." Necessity is the mother of invention; without establishing and convincing students of the necessity of learning the individual objectives it will be that much more difficult for learning to take place. People do what they tend to be interested in. If the teacher does not or cannot develop student interest in the subject matter of the topic objectives, one cannot expect students to learn just because they are told about it, or told to do it. This is one of the greatest challenges the teacher faces; determining how the individual course topic objectives meaningfully relate to the students. If a student is convinced the information presented is needed, then real learning tends to take place. If the student cannot see the need or necessity in the information, they either memorize it or just plain let it go out of the memory window. Overall, it has long been accepted that there is a strong relationship between interest and learning. The teacher must develop "necessity interest" in the student if successful learning is to take place.

CHAPTER REVIEW

Preparation & Presentation: Successful teaching requires the preparation of a Lesson Plan (limited to one page) that is a concise record and location of the planned material to teach, the topic objective, teaching methods (modes of learning), analysis of learning, and improvement.

The Lesson Plan describes the reference material being used to form the contents of the course. The topic objective is the resultant expectation of what is being taught; what the learner should be able to do—measurable. The teaching methods, to be on the receptive wavelength of all students, should be presented multimode—Seeing, Feeling, and Hearing. The Analysis of Learning must determine at what level all the students learned the material and be reviewed for dispersion of the test scores for planning teaching method improvement—if needed. The Lesson Plan is the teacher's guide to ensure and improve student learning.

The foremost challenge of the teacher is not to try to change the students, but to improve the teaching methods which in turn will improve the level of learning of the students.

The first class session is extremely important as it sets the perceptive tone for the entire course. Preparation for the first session should cover all the operational information of the course. It is the teacher's opportunity to establish a supportive learning relationship with the students.

Teachers should expand and compliment textbook information to reinforce the importance of the material being presented. The real responsibility for student learning lies with the teacher's interpretation and created learning experiences to accomplish the textbook intentions.

Developing interest in the subject by showing how the topic objectives meaningfully relate to the students is a continuous and necessary part of course planning.

CHAPTER 3 TASKS

Prepare:

▶ major course information into measurable topic objectives.

▶ a one-page Lesson Plan for a topic objective stating the Reference Material, Topic Objective, Teaching Methods, Analysis of Learning, and Improvement—if needed.

▶ multi-mode ethical Teaching Methods for topic objectives.

▶ Test methods for topic objectives.

▶ an Analysis of Learning (range and dispersion of test grades) for topic objectives

▶ the learning plan's Improvement based on the Analysis of Learning.

Tasks Note: By completing the chapter Tasks, utilizing all three modes of learning, the reader will improve their ability to ensure student learning.

Notes:

Notes: _____

Notes: _____

Chapter 4: Evaluating Learning

The most important purpose of student evaluation is improvement of instruction.

The pre-planning of Topic Objectives, Teaching Methods, and then performing an Analysis of Learning to determine the effectiveness of the teaching methods, determines the need for any improvement. This is the Art and Science of teaching—ensuring learning.

Evaluation

Evaluating student learning is the only logical way a teacher can determine the effectiveness of their teaching. How well have the students learned the material presented by the teacher? Knowing this is necessary to plan teaching methods (modes of learning) that will be more effective for the group being taught. The teaching methods can and probably will change from group to group (class to class) but the necessity of multi-mode teaching versus single mode teaching remains in order to improve student learning. People (students) receive and process information utilizing all three modes of learning, each to their individual mode biases. Some are better receiving information through Seeing, and/ or Doing, and/or Hearing, yet all tend to use all the modes at differing levels (depending on their interest) therefore all three are needed to be most effective in group (classroom) learning. A very experienced educator once quipped: "the variances in the different modes of student learning, and the interest of the individual student at the time of learning, is likened to a dice game aboard the deck of an aircraft carrier during a typhoon." Things change all the time and the best way to prepare for the changing individual modes of learning is to present learning material multi-mode.

Given the variances in learning modes it would appear necessary to evaluate student learning utilizing the various modes although that may not be practical in large classes or time constraints. Evaluation via written answers, checked off multiple choice, etc. evaluates the verbal mode of learning and might appear questionable for evaluating the other multi-modes because the student has to convert the other modes of learned information to a verbal test answer. This may not be as difficult as it appears because the learning has already taken place using multi-modes and only needs to be transferred mentally to answer written questions. The teacher should be able to verbally evaluate the level of learning of all the multi-modes used in learning the material. The goal of evaluation is to determine the level of learning of the teaching methods used, to improve future instruction. A verbal evaluation process should be able to accomplish that.

METHODS OF EVALUATION

What can the teacher devise to evaluate their student's learning of the material, or whatever was presented? If the learning was for verbal communication then the evaluation should be similar—even when all three modes of learning were used. If a mathematical computation, then the assessment should relate to the actual use of the computation in real applications—not just the written/computer completion of an equation—but more so the application of the equation. If a science project or concept, then the application of the concept rather than the verbal definition, etc. All of the above (evaluations) would be a more realistic evaluation of instruction when related to the applications of the concept taught—not just the mechanics, although an understanding of how whatever is derived is essential. This is really evaluating the purposeful outcome of teaching. The actual evaluation method could be an individual assignment, a group problem/solution format, or something that puts the learner in the position of having to correctly apply the multi-mode information received from the teacher.

A paper/pencil/computer test is perceived to accurately assess the student's ability to respond to verbal information retained by all the students. Because most of the students in a class have differing receptive learning biases it would appear to be an inaccurate measure of student learning of the total class, even a class that was taught multi-mode. However, students do convert multi-mode learning to verbal responses based on their memory and interest. Contrarily, if the class was only taught verbally then the traditional student assessment of learning does not relate to multi-mode learners and would appear to be an ineffective measure of learning for that group.

One can see how important it is to teach and assess multi-mode learning for continuing improvement of instruction. *Without multi-mode teaching the teacher will never be able to analyze/determine the inherent learning level capabilities of the student group, or individuals, thus the effectiveness of the teaching methods.*

Multi-mode teaching is most effective but multi-mode testing is not always practical. In many situations verbal testing is the only alternative and should produce evaluations that are accurate enough to determine the level of student learning which then can be used for improving teaching methodologies.

> The purpose of evaluating students
> is to improve instruction.

STUDENT GRADING

Traditional forms of student grading include:

- Letter grades of: P or F: P (passing) F (failing)

- Letter grades of S and N: S (satisfactory), N (needs Improvement)

- Letter grades of O,S,N: O (outstanding), S (satisfactory), N (needs improvement)

- Letter grades of A,B,C,D,F: A (outstanding), B (above average), C (average), D (below average), F (failing).

A typical percentage system for the letter grades of A through F is: A 90-100%, B 80-89%, C 70-79%, D 60-69%, F less than 60%. There are numerous grading systems used in school systems in the U.S. to designate A through F grades, but all are similar in nature to the one described here. Variances most often occur in the percentages assigned to each letter grade.

Sometimes a letter grade of "I" indicates an

Incomplete which has individual school rules for converting to a letter grade.Usually, if not converted within an established time, the "I" grade automatically converts to an F grade.

Letter grading is in common use in the U.S. school system and portrays the student's level of learning of whatever subject/objective it represents. In reality, it portrays the level of learning of the student per the given instruction of the teacher (the teaching method used). Differing teaching methods versus differing modes of student learning will produce varied results, given the same learning objective. That is why student evaluation will really indicate the effectiveness of the instruction and serves as the basis for teaching methods improvement.

Example—No Planning: An elementary school had adopted the "O, S, N" grading policy and during a teacher's conference with a student's parents, the teacher was asked why the parent's child could not receive a letter grade O on her work. They indicated their 2nd grade child was frustrated in that she worked so hard to submit assignments that were correct but was never able to receive an O grade. The teacher responded by saying: "I do not give out O's." It was the teacher's discretion to apply grades and indicated that the only grades attainable were the grades of S or

N. The grade of O was not attainable. The parent was confused.

Note: This is an example of what happens when planning for teaching does not occur. Preplanning topic objectives and teaching methods—then analyzing the learning that took place and improving the teaching methods continuously would improve the levels of learning and allow students to accomplish higher grades. This is better for everyone (students, teacher, parents, school, etc.) *"If preparation is inadequate the results will be poor levels of learning characterized by a number of disruptive student situations."*

GRADING ON A CURVE

Note: There are accepted applications for Curve Grading that are beyond the fundamental teaching concepts promoted in this Handbook, but Grading on a Curve is described for informational purposes as follows:

Grading on a Curve is the process of adjusting test scores in order to ensure a selected grade distribution throughout the class. The actual test scores are adjusted to obtain a desired distribution of grades (generally known as a normal distribution or a normal curve).

In explanation: "The Curve" refers to a bell-shaped curve, recorded on a graph that all student scores are desired to resemble when plotted. The test scoring range is horizontal and the numbers of students attaining those scores vertical. The expectation is: few A's, some B's, many C's, Some D's, and few F's—thus a bell-shaped curve.

An example is distributing 10 percent of whatever the class scores for an A grade, 20 percent for a B grade, 40 percent for a C, and so on. The expectation here is that actual grades are spread out (the grading distribution is pre-determined) to assign grades A's through F's. No matter what the actual test scores are, the grades assigned will be pre-determined by the selected distribution. This grading procedure is *not* useful for continuous improvement in teaching methods because it does not portray the actual level of learning of the objectives tested for each of the students in the class. The effectiveness of the teaching has to be determined by the actual level of learning of the students.

APPLICATION OF CURVE GRADING

Note: An example is presented here to show the advantage of being able to evaluate the learning of topic objectives, to improve the teaching methods, and subsequent learning.

Application: A student was discussing the results

of a test that was taken in a college upper division course (3rd and/or 4th year). The teacher was new to the school and used the Curve Grading system. The student indicated that the test was to be on topics presented in class in the prior weeks. In actuality, the test covered numerous required topics that were never covered in class (nor separately assigned) and as a result the highest score recorded in the class was approximately 40%. The teacher awarded the 40% a letter grade of A. The student who was discussing the results of the test only received a 20% score but was recorded as a B or C grade. In reality, the class evaluation of the material learned was recorded with grades that appeared normal (grade distribution) when actually the level of learning was so low the corresponding grades were incorrect.

The teacher's motive may have been to discover the student's knowledge of material not covered in class, but the subsequent grading was erroneous. Also, this testing did not reveal the level of learning of the topic objectives and thus could not be effective in evaluating and improving the teaching methods and subsequent learning.

EVALUATION FOR IMPROVEMENT

Evaluating students for improvement of teaching methods (modes of learning) can most efficiently be accomplished utilizing the A to F (non-curve) grading system. This easily lends itself to numerical comparisons of learning levels of objectives tested. The comparisons will indicate areas of teaching method improvements needed as well as current successes. Test results indicating a diverse spread of grades, A to F's, is a signal that the teaching methods are not reaching all the students. Some are getting it, and some are not, thus indicating a need for improvement in the teaching methods. Possibly more multi-mode and/or more interest. The challenge of the teacher is to make the teaching method changes that will produce a more straight-line graph plotting A to C rather than the Curve which acknowledges below average level and failure learning.

The goal of improvement is that the learning in the whole class be represented by test results that appear skewed when plotted, indicating A's to C's with minimal (none) down curve to D's and F's. Multi-mode teaching, reaching all the students, should effectively produce results that modify the bell-curve shape and document results of more effective learning for all in the class. Again, this is the challenge of becoming an effective teacher—to evaluate student learning and make the teaching method changes that will improve learning. *"The most important purpose of student evaluation is improvement of instruction."*

In conclusion, it cannot be expected that every student will achieve high grades when teaching to ensure learning although learning will improve immeasurably and the perception of education would be less threatening, more inviting, and ultimately more effective. Teaching to ensure learning is how to significantly improve student learning.

Chapter Review

Evaluating Learning: Evaluation of student learning is the only logical way a teacher can analyze the effectiveness of their teaching. It is well accepted that "the purpose of evaluation is improvement of instruction."

Evaluating students for improvement of teaching methods can most efficiently be accomplished utilizing the A through F (non-curve) grading system. This easily lends itself to numerical comparisons of learning levels of the objectives tested. The grade portrays the level of learning of the student per the given instruction of the teacher (teaching method) indicating the effectiveness of the instruction.

A teacher's goal, depicting student learning, should be a high range of grades, with minimal dispersion, representing the successful level of learning of that respective objective for all students in the class.

Pre planning topic objectives and teaching methods—then analyzing the learning that took place and improving the teaching methods continuously would improve the levels of learning and allow students to accomplish higher grades.

Curve grading is the process of adjusting test scores in order to ensure a selected grade distribution throughout the class. This grading procedure is minimally useful for continuous improvement because it does not portray the actual level of learning of the objectives tested.

Through the process of evaluating learning and subsequent improvement of instruction the student's perception of education would be less threatening, more inviting, and ultimately more effective.

Chapter 4 Tasks

Evaluate Learning by:

► creating tests for course topic objectives.

► grading all tests on a percentage grading scale to identify the actual level of learning of course topic objectives.

► determining any need for improving the teaching methods based on the range of test grades (dispersion of scores) for topic objectives.

Tasks Note: By completing the chapter Tasks, utilizing all three modes of learning, the reader will improve their ability to ensure student learning.

<u>Notes:</u>

Notes:

Notes:

Chapter 5: Eliminating Gender Bias

Gender Bias can negatively influence student course selection and career decisions resulting in too many students not becoming all they are capable of being and/or interested in being.

Gender Bias

GENDER BIAS EXISTS IN MANY forms in the home, school, and the workplace. The problem is that the results of gender bias in schools influence the decisions students make in the courses they take, which in turn influences, and ultimately limits their career choices.

Education statistics indicate there are fewer females in math and science related disciplines because of differences either in social practices between men or women, personal/family obligations, the way math and science are taught in schools, and traditional advisement in schools. Collectively all these situations contribute to the under-representation of females in science related education versus their male counterparts. These situations are serious career determining issues and the more that teachers work to eliminate bias the more career opportunities we open to students, regardless of their gender.

It appears that the seeds of gender bias appear in the shaping of one's mind, similar to programming a computer, from birth and on. We tend to learn what we live and we live what we learn. Unfortunately, some positive intentions done as parents, teachers, role models, etc. have unknowing, unrealistic, and sometimes negative consequences.

GENDER BIAS AT HOME

The social issues begin early in family life with different role expectations between boys and girls. Examples of expectations begin with boys whose expectations are many times perceived and vocalized by their parents to grow up to be in more masculine perceived occupations such as builders, tradesmen, engineers, sports players, etc. Whereas girls are many times perceived and vocalized to grow up to be in more feminine perceived occupations such as models, nurses, secretaries, elementary school teachers, or less masculine fields. These roles, too many times, are self-fulfilling in that individuals try to become what is expected of them.

Unfortunately, what is expected of children is too

many times perceived from tradition rather than logical ability. Girls and boys have similar scholastic abilities yet are steered by biases and tradition rather than generated interest. Additional factors relating to the way gender is differentiated are often times related to geographical norms, religious beliefs, family economics, ethnic and racial backgrounds, etc. It appears that all of these factors tend to promote unbalanced career choices resulting in many students not becoming what they are capable of being, or really interested in being.

GENDER BIAS AT SCHOOL

In school, gender biases tend to increase unnoticed but in themselves are a very strong influence in course and curriculum decision making. Subsequently this influences the student's life altering career decisions.

Gender bias begins in the elementary school and continues to the middle school, and so on. For the most part the coursework developed at these levels is not developed to attract female curiosity. Most lessons presented in the classroom are unknowingly gender biased, as historical contributions made by females in science are not emphasized in the curriculum, versus their male counterparts, nor is the course material presented to accommodate the different learning styles of females.

The first real educational barrier encountered by female students is the challenge of the math and science curriculums. Investigation shows little bias in the early elementary years, but in the middle school, females begin to show a more negative attitude toward math and science than males. This is a glaring example of needing continuous improvement in the more difficult subjects which would then attract students rather than generate the fear that they do. Math and science courses should be designed and taught to generate greater student interest, presented multi-mode to enhance interest and learning, and thus attract more students.

In reality, females in general have fewer science related experiences than males do. Males have a substantially greater history of working with or fixing something mechanical than females do. Overall, females are not exposed to toys and activities that ignite their curiosity about science and tend to be less exposed to science in general. This disinterest in science, and resultant math requirements, leads females to avoid taking the advanced courses necessary for careers in science. When they graduate from high school they are not academically equipped or motivated to pursue careers in science or engineering. Therefore, fewer females enroll in science related programs after they finish high school. It is logical that to lessen/eliminate gender bias in middle and high school curriculums the teachers need to address the interests and learning styles of females. Additionally, the contributions made by women have to be acknowledged in order to maintain female interest. Herein, as most scientists are male, science traditionally has represented a male point of view. Teaching becomes less gender biased when focused more on concerns with social significance and less on specialized mechanical applications. Additionally, solving problems more traditionally female oriented and using less gender biased language allow females to feel less alienated by the process. Examples used in the classroom such as the trajectory of a spacecraft or the mechanical workings of a car are gender biased and few females can relate to the subject matter from prior experience. Because females cannot readily relate to the material, they lose interest and gravitate towards subjects which they feel more relevance.

ADVISEMENT BIAS

Conventional advisement in school has its own biases. Studies of junior high school students show that many male and female students are unaware of career options available to them as well as their educational requirements. Much school advisement and career advisement is predicated on past grades and coursework and this is then used as an inaccurate predictor of future options and success. Thus, many are counseled into traditional career tracks rather than areas of genuine interest, which would necessitate problem solving with the student on how and what to do to achieve interests and goals. As a former statistics professor once indicated: "national studies conducted to follow students from school to work in order to predict outcomes, based on hundreds of variables, could only confidently reveal that boys could lift heavier weights than girls." Any other relationships had minimal levels of significance and were "sheer speculation."

> Student advisement based on past performance is time poorly spent. It is negative because it plants the seed "I can only become something based on what I have already done."

This type of thinking has to be eliminated from teaching. Note that people tend to do well at what they want to do, and the converse seemingly holds true.

ADVISEMENT AND GENDER BIAS

Unfortunately, some schools adhered to traditional advisement norms such as boys take "shop" and girls take "home economics." This is a typical example of illogical and gender biased advisement. This practice, occurring in the not-so-distant past, was practiced by very educated people. Gender bias exists in such simple forms we really do not realize it until we look back and recognize the ignorance of it all.

Example: A traditional advisement bias situation became reality when a female student had to get middle-school board approval to take a "shop" course instead of "home economics." The shop course consisted of one semester of mechanical drawing and the next semester of hands-on producing what was drawn. It was a personal interest decision that defied local advisement norms and required the permission of the school board and its president. The student was just an average young student who had an interest in mechanical arts instead of home economics. She, after significant persistence, received permission only after getting a male student to agree to take her place in the home economics class. Both students had interests differing from advisement norms. This scenario occurred in a middle-school and the female continued through the normal high-school curriculum and then went on to college where she received a B.S. Degree in Mechanical Engineering. Her acceptance of advisement from her college coursework faculty consisted of what courses to take to strengthen her math pre-requisites and was successfully contrary to her high-school adviser's advisement that said "your math background is too insufficient in order to compete in calculus so try a less demanding career." It is apparent that the middle school shop course and her college faculty significantly influenced her career choice and resultant success; contrary to her high school's biased advisement.

TEACHER'S GENDER BIAS

Most teachers themselves are advising students all the time by their perceived actions, statements, looks, demeanor, etc. Teacher gender in itself is a perceived bias because there are significantly more men teaching in math and science at the college level and females feel in the minority for both support and true peer advisement. Conversely there are more females teaching in the elementary system with corresponding effects.

Conventional classroom gender and a lack of role models have a negative impact on female science-oriented students. At the college level, faculty are often required to conduct research and publish in addition to regular teaching duties, therefore females tend to choose a career in industry because it is more compatible with their family life. That is, companies in the world outside of education are more likely to allow women to work part-time. Subsequently, the absence of female faculty for peer support results in less attraction of females into science-oriented curriculums. It is a well-accepted fact that female students tend to seek advisement and peer support from female faculty and, because of that relationship, remain in and successfully complete an academic program that they probably would not have, had there been no female support.

Currently, females comprise approximately 20 percent of the science and engineering labor force in the U.S. but comprise approximately half of the labor force in total. The reasons for this disproportion are certainly diverse but gender bias from home, and including school, are major factors. So, teachers, just being a teacher has a strong gender impact on the perception of students and carries a professional responsibility to promote knowledge and career opportunities emphasizing gender equality.

Chapter Review

Eliminating Gender Bias: Statistics indicate there are fewer females in math and science related disciplines because of differences either in social practices between men and women, personal/family obligations, the way math and science is taught in schools, and traditional advisement in schools.

Collectively, all of these situations appear to contribute to the under-representation of females in science related education versus their male counterparts.

The social issues begin early in family life with different role expectations between boys and girls.

In middle school females begin to show a more negative attitude towards math and science than males. They avoid taking the advanced courses necessary for careers in science.

Examples used in the classroom such as the trajectory of a spacecraft or the mechanical workings of a car are gender biased and few females can relate to the subject matter from prior experience. Because females cannot readily relate to the material as presented, they lose interest and gravitate towards subjects which they feel more relevance.

Conventional advisement in school has its own biases. Advisement appears to focus on past grades and coursework and is commonly used as an inaccurate predictor of future and success.

Student advisement based on past performance is time poorly spent. It is negative because it plants the seed "I can only become something based on what I have already done." This type of thinking should be eliminated from advisement.

Note that people tend to do well at what they want to do, and the converse holds true.

The teacher's gender has a strong impact on the perception of students and carries a professional responsibility to promote knowledge and career opportunities emphasizing gender equality.

CHAPTER 5 TASKS

Eliminate Gender Bias by:

▶ eliminating language in the classroom that promotes perceptions of occupations and successful people by relating to their specific gender.

▶ reducing male gender biased examples used in problem explanations, solutions, and increase female related examples.

▶ increasing, earlier in education, career advisement that focuses on un-biased gender career options and the education requirements to achieve those options.

▶ focusing student advisement on what a student wants to do, and how they can do it, rather than what they are limited to because of their past performance.

▶ increasing female teachers in science and mathematics; serving as both faculty, student mentors, and under-represented role models.

▶ preparing math and science courses presented multi-mode to generate greater interest and attract more students.

Tasks Note: By completing the chapter Tasks, utilizing all three modes of learning, the reader will improve their ability to ensure student learning.

Chapter 5 Reference: Waldheim, Marjorie L. "Comparison of Female and Male Educators," Research Proposal Review of Literature—EDD 596, University of Phoenix

Notes:

Notes:

Chapter 6: Ethics

*A teacher must be both a Manager and a Leader and
has the ethical responsibilities of both positions.*

Teacher Ethics

Ethics are perceived as practicing good conduct
and having moral principles or values. More accurately
the dictionary defines it as the "rules or standards gov-
erning the conduct of members of a profession." This
definitely relates to the teaching profession and thus directly affects student learning. The effect that a teacher's
ethics has on the perceptions learned by students is pro-
lific. One only has to read and study the written student
evaluations of faculty to realize the profound affect the
values of the teacher has on the perception of the students. It is generally discussed by students that there are
few classes taken where the teacher's political views and
other personal values have not been forthcoming. Some
to the extent that it could clearly affect one's relationship
with the teacher and subsequently one's perception of

the grade received.

Faculty projection of personal, political, and/or religious views is a breeding ground for deceptive learning and should be eliminated from the learning environment.

TEACHER RESPONSIBILITIES

It is well accepted in the education profession that the teacher is both the Manager and the Leader in the classroom and should conduct themselves at the highest level of perceived values. Remember, students are learning from the teacher's perceived actions as well as their words. Personal views and actions relating to religion, politics, morality, and other controversially potential subjects should be avoided unless they are an integral part of the course being taught.

Where controversial subjects are a required part of the course, and discussed, it is the teacher's responsibility to present both sides of the issue with the intent of providing enough non-biased information so students can make their own judgments and decisions in a non-biased atmosphere.

In practice it appears that "ethics" seems to be a subject in teaching practice and evaluation that is generally avoided until a problem occurs and then critics refer to the obvious "ethical professional responsibility" of the person or whatever in question, after the occurrence. One only has to read the continual media reports of public teachers being involved in conduct contrary to their professional responsibilities. This type of non-ethical behavior has no place in education because it is the teacher's professional responsibility to *always* set a positive example of character and values.

The following description just about sums up ethics in education: A teacher must be both a Manager and a Leader. The manager of the classroom environment and the leader of the subject/group being taught. The ethical responsibilities of both positions are well defined by the paraphrase: "Managers must do things right—Leaders must do the right things."

> "Managers must do things right—
> Leaders must do the right things."

CHAPTER REVIEW

Where controversial subjects are a required part of the course, and discussed, it is the teacher's responsibility to present both sides of the issue with the intent of providing enough non-biased information so students can make their own judgments and decisions in a non-biased atmosphere.

It is well accepted in the education profession that the teacher is both the Manager and the Leader in the classroom and should conduct themselves at the highest level of perceived values.

Chapter 7 Reference: AAUP (American Association of University Professors) Policy Documents and Reports, eleventh edition.

Chapter 6 Tasks

Practice Ethics:

▶ Personal views and actions relating to religion, politics, morality, and other controversially potential subjects should be avoided unless they are an integral part of the course being taught.

▶ Where controversial subjects are a required part of the course, and discussed, it is the teacher's responsibility to present both sides of the issue with the intent of providing enough non-biased information so students can make their own judgments and decisions in a non-biased atmosphere.

▶ Where the teacher is both the Manager and the Leader in the classroom and should conduct themselves at the highest level of perceived values.

Tasks Note: By completing the chapter Tasks, utilizing all three modes of learning, the reader will improve their ability to ensure student learning.

Notes:

Notes:

Chapter 7: Teaching Tasks to Accomplish

The text presents information verbally thus completion of the Tasks are designed to involve the reader in the learning modes of Seeing and Feeling making the learning experience of the text multi-mode.

Chapter 1 Tasks

Create:

- genuine student interest in all course topics and abolish threats of any kind.

- all three effective learning modes for teaching each course topic.

- evaluations (tests) to measure and analyze student learning of course topics.

- improvement in teaching methods—if needed.

- a classroom perception that the teacher's primary priority is student learning.

Chapter 2 Tasks

Plan how to:

- accept the fundamental teaching responsibility of student learning.
- combine abstract learning and training of course topics.
- improve student retention.
- improve learning reinforcement.

Chapter 3 Tasks

Prepare:

- major course information into measurable topic objectives.
- a one-page Teaching Plan for topic objectives stating the Reference Material, Topic Objective, Teaching Methods, Analysis of Learning, and Improvement—if needed.
- multi-mode ethical Teaching Methods for topic objectives.
- Test Methods for topic objectives.
- an Analysis of Learning (range and

dispersion of test grades) for topic objectives.

- the learning plan's Improvement based on the Analysis of Learning.

CHAPTER 4 TASKS

Evaluate Learning by:

- creating tests for course topic objectives.

- grading all tests on a percentage grading scale to identify the actual level of learning of course topic objectives.

- determining any need for improving the teaching methods based on the range of test grades (dispersion of scores) for topic objectives.

CHAPTER 5 TASKS

Eliminate Gender Bias by:

- eliminating language in the classroom that promotes perceptions of occupations and successful people by relating to their specific gender.

- reducing male gender biased examples used in problem explanations, solutions, and increase female related examples.

- increasing (earlier in education) career advisement that focuses on un-biased gender career options and the education requirements to achieve those options.

- focusing advisement on what a student wants to do, and how they can do it, rather than what students are limited to because of their past performance.

- increasing female teachers in science and mathematics; serving as both faculty, student mentors, and under-represented role models.

- preparing math and science courses presented multi -mode to generate greater interest and attract more students.

CHAPTER 6 TASKS

Practice Ethics:

- personal views and actions relating to religion, politics, morality, and other potentially controversial subjects should be avoided by teachers unless they are an integral part of the course being taught

- where controversial subjects are a required part of the course, and discussed. It is the teacher's responsibility to present both sides of the issue with the intent of providing enough non-biased information so students can make their own judgments and decisions in a non-biased atmosphere.

- where the teacher is both the Manager and the Leader in the classroom and should conduct themselves at the highest level of perceived values.

Notes:

Notes:

Notes:

About the Author

The author, Dr. George P Waldheim, spent the first half of his career in private business and the second half in public education. Formal education includes an Associate Degree from Erie County Technical Institute (currently Erie Community College) Williamsville NY, Bachelor and Master of Science Degrees in Education from Buffalo State College, State University of New York (SUNY) Buffalo NY, Doctorate in Education from the University at Buffalo (SUNY) Buffalo NY.

The author began teaching in the Military, afterward teaching and administering a wide variety of classes from church school to two-year College, four-year College, and then the University. Positions included: Sergeant– US Marine Corps Training Command. Co-owner of a Manufacturing Company in Buffalo NY. Associate Professor at the University of Nebraska-Omaha/Lincoln NE. Professor and Department Chair at California State University-Chico CA. Dean of Business and Technology at College of the Redwoods-Eureka CA and Dean of the College of Technology at Ferris State University-Big Rapids MI. Personally, the author and his wife parented two children from kindergarten to college to the world of work.

The author's service includes: Rotarian Eureka CA. President Small Business Development Center (SBDC) Humboldt and Del Norte Counties CA. Vice President CA Community Colleges Association of Occupational Education (CCCAOE) North/Far North Region. Chair CA North Coast Articulation Council. Regional Accreditation Reviewer for Northwest Association of Schools and Colleges-Seattle WA.

Awards include Award of Excellence for outstanding achievement in education, research, and service to students *"Teacher of the Year"* by the College of Engineering & Technology, Halliburton Education Foundation, University of Nebraska-Omaha/Lincoln. "Professor Emeritus" Award. California State University-Chico. North Coast Small Business Center, Service Award, Eureka, CA.

Prior Professional Memberships: Society of Manufacturing Engineers (SME). Chair American Society for Engineering Education (ASEE) Midwest Section Engineering Technology Division. National Association of Industrial Technology (NAIT).

www.ingramcontent.com/pod-product-compliance
Lightning Source LLC
Chambersburg PA
CBHW041818090426
42811CB00009B/1014